How I See
The World

How I See The World

M. Rayne

To order additional copies of this book, contact:
Xlibris
1-888-795-4274
www.Xlibris.com
Orders@Xlibris.com
815209

" 🕊️ Broken 🕊️ "

Why are all my loved ones dying around me

No sideshow, then why are all these clowns found still around me

Thirteen is supposed to be a bad luck number

But for me it's not, it's a reflection of you

It was our introduction, before knowing we were cousins

An uninformed jersey worn inception of our youth

Before you became who you were, you was just to me a cool kid

Had the biggest heart, intelligent, charismatic, but never had a beef started, provoked or condoned any static

That was you, calm but turned up when it was time to party

Never once witnessed nor heard about your involvement in anything illegal, hardly

Haha, I can laugh at it now, looking back

I'm tearing up now writing this, and thinking back to the days, cooking up the hits in the lab, listening to the tracks

You inspired me, (little did you know), to go hard in my writing, by listening and vibing to your wordplay, delivery, and rhyme schemes like a Titan

The track about your daughter is the hardest one of all

Not because I'm on it with you, but because it was true words from the heart.

Take me off the song, and it's a still classic,

I want the world to hear.

You said exactly how every father feels bout their daughter, but you did it effortlessly, with conviction, I'm being sincere.

The fact that you're no longer here with us, that will forever hurt

I'm still shaking my head, feeling like it's a bad dream, knowing that denial of truth never works

My heart goes out to your family, and cause they feel what I feel, an emptiness inside

I had more plans for us musically
just waiting for things to align

And now that you're gone, I keep hearing," he's in a better place"

When all I feel is the better place is here with all of us, seeing his face

Hearing his laughter, tripping off his jokes that he would make

Somebody tell me, why him or anybody that I love

I need answers, cause to me, this is reminiscent to being pushed off a building without a parachute before the plunge

Life isn't fair, that I already knew

But damn, the strangest things makes no sense, guess I have to learn that too

Why this way, was it something I said
is it my fault, that this creative soul was taken away

My pain will be eternal, this is too much to bear

If this happens again, I'm going too, that's the way that I feel....©

"Injustice"

(IN JUST US)

These institutions jails and prisons,

Can't survive if people stop committing crimes to get locked up in them.

In the streets,

Young Brothers get disrespected, now he makes plans to line up his victim.

Another body dead in the streets.

No witnesses or no leads just an outcry of help from police, flashing tip lines across TV screens

But no one dares not snitch, unless they want their house tatted with infrared beams. Awakened to hearing screams.

Bullets flying through screen doors, windows, and crashing through figurines.

A horrific explicit version of an attempted murder scene

Baltimore, Maryland better known as Bodymore, Murderland

Where you can get killed coming out of your front door, or shot while serving up grams

Here, this is an urban revised version of the new "300"

Where each year the murder rate is no less than 300

Too many parents, have had to bury their kids, before they reach the age of 13

Parental dreams shattered for coming to graduations or, hanging up college degrees.

Men and women pay attention,

We're wiping out our own race. Melanated brothers and sisters, no fiction, we're turning into victims or a Cold Case.

Jails and prisons are overcrowded, and the beds keep getting filled.

When we all should be at home in bed, getting ready for work, and when you're not working, you're at home on chill.

Fighting court cases like a 12-round heavyweight bout Hoping that the state's attorney doesn't catch you with a punch, that knocks you out.

Whether paid lawyer or public defender, it really don't matter.

They'll be sitting at dinner, discussing your case, conversing, cursing and laughing.

While you're locked in your cell, biting your nails, thinking about what happened.

The way I see it, if you get charged and locked up, they call it justice But people, we need to smarten up, we're the only ones...

In_ Just_ Us

"The Switch"

Order, order in the Court, now young man would you like to say something?

Yes, in fact I do your honor, now let's reverse the basics.

Dress you in this yellow suit, shackles, adorn you with these bracelets.

While you're riding back to the jail, mad as hell, about the whole situation.

This is really amazing, couldn't even get pretrial release or probation.

Next you go from the van to the jail, and then to the elevator, still shocked in amazement.

Oh but it gets better, welcome to your residential housing for placement.

This here is a 25 2 a room tier, where a sign of fear could mean imminent danger.

Bullets for bangers, domestics, and murderers, are just some amongst the many that's nameless.

Only four phones for everybody to conversate with loved one's, completely brainless.

Whomever's idea it was to only put four phones on the tier, should be shot for everybody's entertainment.

My bad, I digress, let me get back to the business of your orientation.

This is a 22 by 2 lockdown tier.

Three meals a day, and no one except the "working man" comes out on Wednesdays.

Unless by any chance, someone has put money on your books, and you order commissary.

Now the next lessons important, stop looking around and pay attention.

Keep your hands to yourself, stay in your lane, and mind your business.

If you need something, ask for it, you steal it, you get what you ask for.

A good old-fashioned passionate, elaborate, never get tired, ass whooping, cuz you asked for it.

I know for you this is a strange change in perspective.

See the faces in here, you put them here, to learn their lesson.

The look on your face, is going to be met with shear aggression.

Terrorized and petrified, scared to die, like you're floating in an ocean, not knowing sharks smell blood in seconds.

No more can you hide behind the bailiff and the gavel.

From the day room to your cell, that's as far as you can travel.

The room that you're in, makes you feel like you're boxed in, like the walls grew life and about to close you in.

Stay on your pivot because, you got to be here, at least 30 days for a visit.

By that time, you'll be so scared, when you see them, you're begging, "get me out this instant".

Now that was a little depiction of my life in jail.

If you ever have to step in between these doors, you'll hear the Lion's roar screaming "Welcome to HELL"!!!!

"Clocks Ticking"

Is it the color of my skin that delegates the circumstances of my life?

A wasted probation to hasten life, and my place in it by discombobulation.

Another cover that dims the shine of my light, the soundtrack to my life.

As the darkness falls, the frustration is born.

Adjacent blatant navigations to mental depictions of world wind thrills and chills, and my complacent existence due to the scrupulous redacted contusions and lack of intervention...

Watch me grab the proverbial metal for battle, through metaphors I travel in light speed, I speak, strong words of wisdom, though not weak, but in pain I might be...

The struggle is realer than most of y'all can conceive, though easy for most of y'all to conceive, but the birth of a new idea, which may not work, is hard for all to bear and believe.

Though you give it your all, whatever that may be, try, try again, that's what I hear before the setting scene of grief.

Crunch time, now what do you do?

Throw in the towel, slump down in a corner and cry, all while flipping the bird at the world, silently screaming Fuck You, to all who coulda, woulda, but didn't...

Feeling so alone and distant... Heart turning colder than an Alaskan morning, and a Montana Christmas.

I'm not to blame for this life I'm in.

It was not my idea to be this pissed off, this mentally thrown off,

Although strange things, breeds crazy dreams. But desperation leads to aggravation, which ultimately culminates into a very dark mental basement...

Ahhh, candles out, as I hear the blowing of the wind.....

"No Time"

Time.......tics away....clocks displays.... Time

Minutes and seconds of everyday

So many lives enslaved in... Time.....

Time is of the essence

A blessing for some, to others a gun

A sequential bullet slowed down

By invisible hands around the sun

Setting and rising, nightfalls and moonlighting/in the eyes of children they look at the glare of the moon in amazement, but to their sustainment

It only means that bedtime has arrived

And to stay up there's no more....Time...

Numbers forever moving movements

Conducive to moves meant in good faith or bad purpose, in which the worthless misfortune of horrid proportion

Which forces those with dark hearts and sinister intentions to be arraigned upon apprehension, through court systems, while sisters in court shed tears of sadness, rather than joy, all because the judge gave a brother all that.....time.....

If eyes are a window to the soul then time must be a door to life.

Time runs fast, time moves slow,

Time waits for no man, time to go.

Time to make the donuts, time to show

Time is a hot commodity an oddity, and oddly its a facade, that's meant to control you, your movements, your go here and gotta get there, and can't be late for that punctual dinner dates

The oscillation of fluctuations

Spent around on a spindle of windows

In global rotation, for some its a gift for others its a curse, but either way you spin it, it can't all be reversed

So grateful should be, those who have time, for if you don't have time, then this means that your clock has expired....

If only we all could turn back the hands of time, what would we reverse, and how far would you unwind, the ties that binds the confined, and the blind, who once had a vivid vision, but now just darkness in their eyes, only if they had....time..©

"Reversal of Thought"

It's crazy how a split second can alter your life

Words to live by, witness my burdens of strife

Unnerving conversions like when birds switch directions in flight

A plan not planned, on command, autopilot by sight

I stand ten toes like a famed grandmother

Arm leg, leg, arm, head, arm wear bezel

Diabolical logistics, logical thoughts of a misfit,

Cause n effects wit no witness

Doused and effected by quick flips

Attitudes and aptitudes hand and hand in direction

Cohesive agreements desecrated by false corrections

Vest up, or start investing, prepare for the worse

The future is not promised to those who don't understand what it's worth

Their worth or the worth of the creativity within

Which needs to be harnessed, garnered, mastered, and financially metastasized, to create a large profitable margin

The greatest feats in the world we're accomplished by those who failed to see, that they were impossible

Achieved, and later believed, perceived by the masses to whatever obstacle

My mental inoculation is to spread this honest agent

Cleansing of the mental by physical means is almost flagrant

Never too basic, disconnected and discombobulated by ignorant decisions and revisions that alter your situation

Now faced with and without choices to progress your life's cataclysmic conditions, by condolences during, reprieve or bereavement and grieving conversational retention

In this life, I'm faced with a menagerie of thoughts

Though I try to evade them

Cerebral upheaval scares me to death, adjacent to a face to face meeting with Satan

Cerebellum running laps in a match I can't win

Never heard the gun go off,

As I look up, I'm in dead last again

Won't be trapped again

When does the good life really begin?

Depression, frustration, and anger had decided to drive, won't you get in.

Oh don't mind them, they're the drivers next of kin

Happiness, n joy took a backseat just to fit in, better yet sit in, and watch as the melee unfolds

Hopefully frustration won't turn to hatred, as the story is told

Another site to behold, nothing good ever comes from that

More extension of pretentious get backs, set backs, and verbal heinous attacks

I'm so berated at that

How elation can mean a step forward

While separation means a step back

Woo watch my step back

James Harden with the shot

Put up or shut up

Just one of the many lessons I was taught

Be careful of the finer things that catch your eye

Beauty is only skin deep

But ugliness rears its head for a nasty surprise

A bat from an eye, a smug, a smirk, or grin

Just a visual collision, waiting for your acknowledgement

With representative in place, the stage is set

Adjacent to a scene in Undercover Boss, will the character be too soon discovered, and his match finally met

Who knows what lies ahead, in this matrix called life

The elites beat feet and retreat to safe havens amidst the commotion and strife

While the rest of us, are left to rot, and ruin each other, by acts of desecration in fights

This can't be life

It's gotta be a better way to survive

Oh yeah, one more thing

If dying is easy, then why is living so hard

If loving is life, then why are there so many, wounded, bruised battered and broken, feeling hopeless, covered by mental scars... Word to the wise

To love, is to renounce hate...in this mental fight while we're all in... Deep State,©

"Mental Decapitation"

Torn up, ripped to shreds

Lacerated, wished him dead

Eviscerated with hatred

Degradation hastens his death

Mental capacity hap hazardous savagery, tragic catastrophe

Bludgeoned n bashed random antics of maniacal mastery

Heart broken, like cars choking it stopped coasting

Exhaust with the frost, in parts of the part, that ain't suppose to start smoking, he watches hoping, Inflamed with the pain that bangs like scars when propped open

Memory immortally dismembered, No true intention, his conditional focus

Worsens from verbal corrosion

Sick from an expired dosage

Afflicted and twisted visions

Sadistic depictions of wicked

Emotions, potions so potent

Elixir administered, hinders his motions, Ostracized though mentally prophesized, view the commotion, potentially potent potions, paralyzing narrow minded promotion

Devotions remoted motions

Not to those who can even quote it

It's worthless n severely hopeless

Cold cases remain frozen

Brain waves filled with the same concoction

Embedded in a junkies syringe

Before the poken

Mentally coasting

Galactic excursion

So ahead of my time

I have to look back to see when I wrote this

Words, and thoughts of a lonely soul

Without sound I blast away

Until the next life, when I choose

My untimely resurgence...

"Desecration of the Mind"
(Mental Assault)

In case anyone hasn't noticed

There's been a multitude of transitions that need focus

It is so many, I don't know where exactly to start

So allow me to try to dissect sections of the mental molesting

That's been subjected to everyone by ears, eyes and an open heart

The music that's promoted and used, is an evil industry's way to control the hidden innocence of our youth

I call it the dumb down effect, or stupid is the new smart

Idiotic lies that's been told, to try to unfold, and pry the control

From hard working parents hands that has the drive to keep striving to guide their young to one day become something more than just dumb

A parent I am, apparently apparent we care that there's a soul in our children hidden and consumed by "do it for the vine", ratchet fights, and any other entity

That really is ridiculous, infused and hell bent on reeking havoc on the mental state of the world

In short, to all parents, if you're having any difficulties with your kids

And it seems you have tried all you can and given all you could give

Don't blame yourself for not being able to be victorious in your plight

The blame falls on insidious puppeteers for the "Desecration of the Mind"......

"The Matrix"

Patience takes time

With time comes patience

Make sure that you learn something, from every lesson that you're faced with

Lies, gossip, and being back stabbed by close friends is all basic

Pain don't even hurt no more, it's all painless

What hurts the most, is who did it

And the motive behind the hatred

Stand ten toes with all the real ones

The fakes get a facelift

Elevated to the sky, no flight plan or plane trips

If others wanna jump in on your behalf, they get the same trip

Doctors, ICU, or pall bearers, bearers appalled

While they're crying, viewing you faceless, dead weight, and brain dissolved

The "sheeple" of this world remain living

With eyes wide shut

Some choose not to see the truth,

Even if it's standing right in front of them

The facts are there to find, if you do the research is done without hesitation.

Some may say these are controversial, and conspiracy theory filtered statements.

My retort would be, that everyone is entitled to there own belief and opinion, no matter how blatant.

But what is true and fact based, is that we ALL are systemically stuck in this universal system of things I call,

THE MATRIX

"Simple and plain"

Niggaz attract bitches

Gentlemen attract ladies

Role reversal equivalent to hospitals and newborn babies

Gospel rhythms and riddles ridiculous

Lessons learned through quotations

Relationships and love-making

Adjacent to sensual sex faces

Ain't it crazy, we're all in a race war

Where there's really no winner

Society's about lies being told

Controversy, senseless killings of innocent victims

We'll never know if Trayvon Martin and Mike Brown could've been friends

Or if, Amadou Diallo was really followed while minding his business

It's sickening, and this is supposedly the great country that we live in

Where court cases are televised black or white, to draw the highest t.v. ratings for Benjamin's

Dividends divided like pies and fed to the middlemen

Ahh yes..the middlemen,

Chosen for the dastardly deeds

To orchestrate and deliver grisly scenes

Of an evil degree for unlimited green

So I say THINK people, it's not illegal yet

I'm gon feed you this thought,

It shouldn't be hard to digest

When there's controversy on t.v.

Or something so bad on the news

Start to wonder why "they"

Spend so much time on the subject

But more importantly, what else

"They" are really trying to do.......

"Loves pain"

One heart meets another

Single to mingle, a meet and greet sparks another

Third time a date is requested, she's hesitant at first but soon after consideration, elated she accepts it

In preparation for date night, she showers and powders her face right

Fumbles through her closet, for an outfit that'll fit her waist right and light up his eyes like brake lights

Once she's slipped it on, time to comb her silky hair

Throw on some dazzling earrings, just to give the outfit flare

Now satisfied with her decadent ensemble,

Off to start the date today, that could potentially be her tomorrow

Things going great, there's attraction between the two

Which now leads to quiet evenings, and a love affair blazing anew

Days and months have passed, feelings now on full blast

Blazing like candles and volcanoes overflowing sulphuric gas

She's... head over heels, he's in over his head

He never thought that a few compliments, and outings meant that moving in together would lead her to everyday be in his bed

He hates being smothered, and she loves to be up under him

His boys texting and calling, come to the bar so we can kick it

He runs it by her, she sulks and says, "ok but don't be late

I'm cooking your favorite, Mac-n-Cheese and Fried Chicken"

He says "I won't baby, see you later"

She...has reservations bout the friends that he's gon drink with

He's...anticipating that just being around his friends again

Upon being there for well over an hour, he receives many texts from lady love at home, and puts his phone on silent

Already four beers in, he's unknowingly being watched

His boys points out a potential temptress, that should be considered a "Thot"

But boys will be boys, and soon a challenge is made

"I bet you can't book her before she leaves" is what one of them said

Instead of elatedly telling the crew of the new love he's found

He accepts the bets, steps to the left, and proceeds to meet her now

They exchange pleasantries, he smiles, she's wowed, and soon after they leave ...Bad decisions usually lead to worse conditions, but some men never ever take heed

Upon leaving, he waves bye to his crew, But little does he know a friend of lady loves was in the back of the bar, snapping pics, shaking her head while sipping Merlot 6 hours later, he wakes up hangover in tow

No shoes on and clothes sprawled, all over the floor

Alone in a room without any knowledge of how he got there

Casually he staggers to the bathroom, to gather himself and get some fresh air

When he notices through perspiration, some words drawn on the foggy mirror written in rouge lipstick

It read," BUSTED" NEVER TRUST A BIG BUTT N A SMILE

He's thinking WTF is this shhh

He soon discovers his wallet and keys are missing

There's numerous condom wrappers and used busted rubbers as he clears his vision, he thinks for a minute it had to be the girl that I left with, same dame who changed lanes is the prime suspect for the events sealed with a death kiss

No time to ponder that, gotta split to where home is at

Two more hours til sunrise, he starts to devise a lie which will revive faith in lady loves eyes for him like when they met the for the first time

To his surprise upon getting out the cab, she's up, awake, pacing and waiting

He's nervous, and worried what she's thinking

Instinctively he says, "hey sorry I'm late, had car trouble and wouldn't you know it, locked my keys and phone in it rushing to get to the bar, while they were serving free doubles"

That was followed by the previous nights events in an elaborate explanation

And after that, there was a dead silence, like death bells in your ear, from being in a loud club with the speaker banging

She then casually replies, "you must be tired, have a seat, I'll be back baby"

A few moments stray, and she returns with a box, while slowly pacing

She places it on the table, and cool as a fan starts to snicker

He's...perplexed and says," what's this", and she replies

"Man I thought you were going to be different"

Stunned by her response, but shocked to ask what she meant by that statement, he opened up the box and the look on his face was utter disbelief and amazement.

For the contents inside were that of which he recognized

His wallet, keys and even the kind of condoms he had inside

And if that were not enough, when you thought it couldn't get any worse

She called out a name, and in walked a familiar face that all but killed the excuses he had conjured up at first

You see honey dip at the bar a.k.a the "Thot" was really paid to play the game and expose him by any means and in every way she could concoct

And with evidence against him, he just shook his head

But she was passed a revolver by the "Thot"

Lady love said to him, "you were suppose to be the one my very first love for the rest of my life, my everything"

"What did I do that was so wrong to you, that would make you want to kill me inside like this", she screamed

He proceeded to fake grieve, beg and plead.

But revenge was on her mind, not entertaining his infinite pleas

So finally she wiped the abundance of tears from her soft face

Aimed the revolver, to solve and end all of the problems

POW!!!! She shot the "Thot" first, straight to the head

He was scared, looking on in awe of the situation he created

She exclaimed, can't have no witnesses to this type of pain

No one will be able to tell this story, no judge, prosecution, defense and no jury

Then she takes aim at him and says, "You were and will always be mine"

And with that said, she ended his life

Shortly after that, she slid close to his frame, regretting what she had done

Held him close, with revolver enclosed pointed to her temple, and squeezed the trigger, and her last thoughts were no more......

Blurred vision and pain is what he felt in a sense

His chest was a mess, his shirt was bloody and drenched

Two bodies laid softly on the floor

A horrific crime scene to see

It was supposed to have been a third victim, but a bad long distance shot was the reason why he didn't meet his maker, during this plot

So after all this, there really was a witness, you see.

Who lived to tell the tale of a crazy night involving us three?

How do I know?...

Well the reason why I know you see, because I was the third victim

Yes that...was me......

"So Much More"

How do you apologize to someone who means more to you then breathing?

How do you fix what's been broken like a chest compressed by coughing n wheezing?

Can a heart be renovated n restored back to its original state of grace without a sign of bereavement?

Will there ever be a time, designed to refine and align these two minds, with potential positive pretenses, bombarded in sequences of events past n present, ending in a celebratory achievement?

To them it may mean less, but for me this is a way to relieve stress, and the pain, I've felt, by the pain I've dealt, to you are incomparable, believe me

A beautiful flower, whose smile is likened to a shimmering shower of angelic love and true devotion, a powerful potion, once sipped, it courses through a body like coasters

Rolling, swirling seemingly as a smooth summers wave, erupting like a volcanoe, but usually comedic, collected, and equipped with a unique personality that's infectious...

To "them", it may mean nothing, but to me, its so much more...©

"The Real World"

I am one man who verbally vocalizes, for the young n old

I speak what's not spoken, believe n breathe what's not told

The degrees of my mentality, exceeds speeds conceived, on
a limitless Autobon, as I continue to debate "real" t.v.

why, oh you're surprised/allow me to break it down in Pi's
see, the shows that's shown, shows glamorous glitzy lives
a dream to make millions on t.v.,to be
televised/to tell ill advised lies

your life is now privatized/ but it is no longer your own
it is now bought, rewritten, re-thought, and
given to the masses like many souls sold

how many souls behold, the naked truths
that refuses to be clothed in robes

unmask the veil of deceit and lies, which lies to
deceive through media wires across the globe

government schemes scam nations, they own
information pertinent to our salvation

The news nowadays consists of more sex, crimes, and violence

The same thing that's shown on most t.v. shows and premier pilots

As tears form under my eyelids, many thoughts come to my mind
We live in a nation, that hates us, and makes it hard to survive

Years ago, mom and dad, only had to have one job to make it

Now let's face it, we're in a New World Order of enslavement

More work with no sleep, working to pay
bills, and spend more for less to eat

The pestilence is here, and famine is hazardly the
seeking the meek for a weakening defeat

Everyday we're being hit with Silent Weapons,
while Quiet Wars are concocted

By the time many minds, come to grips and
realize who's the REAL hostage

It'll be obvious, be cautious
The end will begin, with the loss lives, of
many men, women and children

The elite will retreat, swiftly to underground buildings

And this is the world we live in, the Real World I tell you

Stay tuned as I conclude more truths, in The Real World part II

Heed my warnings, the beast is among us, waiting
to enslave us, concentration camp ruckus...

"Deep Thought"

Stress is a test that's passed and failed

Many people never try to devise or prioritize their lives

In a manner where its simplified, so they won't prevail

Living in a world where problems
and complications are all too common

To solve them is a resolve
in which it takes time and may be even costly

An awesome division to add may multiply your life

So no one and nothing has to be subtracted while your evolving

Honestly life is just a chess game

I surmise in time

If the right moves are made, and your
defense holds against the opposition

There will be nothing you can't accomplish

All it takes is faith and a vision!

"As I Tremble"

Love is a feeling of excitement

A likeness of vibrance tightness, a vice grip hold of your heart

As it beats like blows from a night stick

A commitment of passionate confinement

Divided with divisional differences

Provisions or a silence

Passions explode and implode with force from a hydrant

Turned on full blast spewing out of control

Right from the beginning or behind closed doors

There's an "APB" for this mysterious L.O.V.E.

It's responsible for deployment of pain, anguish, joy, though sometimes vanquished

Then other times it disappears quickly, speeding off in a Vanquish

Aston Martin, I'm sorry, my condolences for the loss hearts

That's been left scarred and dearly departed by the degradation

Relinquished on a population populated, with ostentatious propagations

Some hate it, and debate it, but everyone has not evacuated the search for love

For the ones who has had their fun, and the ones whose been had by the fun time

Some contrive to run by games for unbiased reasons, they do not know

How much love can love you back, or can be exquisitely deceiving

By men and women who harbor I'll fated relentless reasons to

Asphyxiate others by treason, and insanity beyond reason.....

Belief is a choice, your choice of what to believe in...©

"Thoughts Never Spoken"

Two angels were sitting there waiting to be seen

Both had questions about life's issues, and what they really mean

So, all of a sudden one of them looked over to the other one and said," hey can we have a discussion, there's no need to be fussing,

I mean your views maybe different from mine, but we can agree to disagree, no need for no cussing".

The other angel said," sure, absolutely but I need to implore, you do know what my line of work consists of, in other words who it is that I work for"?

"Sure", the other angel replied, "but you also know who I'm employed by too, don't you"

The second angel nodded his head, and with that being said, the discussion in transition soon after began.

The first angel said," you know the world is already in shambles, every year there's more deaths, cover-ups, turmoil, and scandals

So, my question to you is, "how can a government control a country, hell bent on destruction, and have the audacity to punish their own population, with lies, conspiracies, and unlawful monetary reductions"!

The 2nd second angel paused and thought for a second, taken aback the by severity of the question, but in awe of the facts stated, in the unscrupulous way possible, he began his rebuttal in dramatic fashion infused with biased emotional satirical traction.

He begins," why that answer is quite simple, the rulers of that planet couldn't care less

Their only main concern, is to tighten nooses around all necks

Implant chips and batteries in all flesh

No matter race, religion, or sex, to them nothing else matters regardless

Family ties are being severed, as young men, who are sons and brothers prepare to sign up to intervene in a scheme constructed by the ones that funded the war that's governed

Meant to be destroyed, by greed their all deployed, most won't make it back, looked at as a casualty of war

Mother's lives shattered forever mentally mourning, memories of loved ones, who was commanded and sent to be tortured

I could go on and on with facts of enforcement, but for now I'll quiet down and relinquish to you the floor again

The first angel said," wooo, that was intense.

You know for a split second while you were describing, the sequence of events, I could clearly see them, and my heart started to weaken, weeping, bleeding deeply in a distance

Then in an instance, he said," I still have a menagerie of questions to ask, and hopefully you answer them, and my questions will end in a successful non-stressful bombardment with me saying no mas'!!!

"Is there a race war brewing that the government is trying to construct through futile yet frugal conventions construed through hostile intentions"?

Emphatically, the second angel said," why yes, isn't by now quite obvious to you all"? "If you pay attention to the writing on the wall, pause for the clear view, then you will be able to see through the smoke and the fog"!

"What I'm saying is this business (I meant country),

like the industry is all a game, and the humans are the ones who's being played. It's designed also by those that control the game, and the intricacy of moves that are made."

With a serious look on his face, and a feeling of utter disgrace, the first angel said," well, can you explain how to win the game, and or the basics, in other words break free from the scheme in this matrix"?

Cunning and inconspicuously, he answered," if I gave you all of the answers to any test, than how can you then learn the difference between better, or best?

"The true answers cannot be found through our employers.

"It can only be found in those that seek the power to learn the truth and what can destroy us"

And with that, the two parted, as if they were summoned by two callings, never to meet again, like a changed man who pays in dollars

It's funny how one conversation, can start a whole movement, through moves meant to captivate mind frames, mental unions.

People do your due diligence, we all need to unite, and take back our rights

Or what good is there being a boxer, when nobody starts to fight....

"My Perspective"

In the city that I live in,

It's hard to survive working 1 9-5

Good jobs requires criminal records to be clean, to get hired

So many young brothas, rapping and trapping just tryna survive

That's the dope Boyz, gun totin, cutcha throat Boyz, ski mask, gloves
and rope Boyz

Kidnapping ransom note Boyz

Where the only way out is 3 ways

A wicked jump shot, mic skills, or D.O.A.

So many mamas, and grand mama's cry to the Lord

When a barrage of bullets fly, and a child is involved

Are we dying to live, or living to die

We don't get the chance, to make that decision in life

Living in a world full of sin, filled with sinister plots

We're just pawns in a chess game, checkmate, now punch the clock

Game over, brush my shoulders, hold my scrotum and my head high

R.I.P. to my son Najaad and my grandmother Gloria Brice

She paid the price, when I was young, I use to wreck your nerves

One Republic, "Apologize", Floetry,

If I Was A Bird"

I would fly away, from all this pain and misery

Sometimes I feel I'm trapped in a world, with no lights to see

It seems, that once again, I've become my own worst enemy

An enemy of myself, a battle of good and evil deep inside

Where the weak, withers away, and the strong survives

Is there really a heaven, cause I'm living in hell

Since "98", I'm living a life that's not mine, too much to tell

But hopefully soon, my reconciliation should be coming

I want my life back, Gary Coleman, "Different Strokes", Phil Drummond

"Pain"

The rage within, that hastens the engagement to sin

Embracing the basic basics, that it takes to pace me to win

Evade the name change and blame game, as flagrant degradation begins

Separate from the main frame

,so your segregated from an optically enabled cable lens

Discombobulation of ligaments

and bones, fractured with cracked ribs, will easily set the tone

Punctured lung no words won't come from, a larynx severed next, rotator cuff slammed hard like receivers on phones

On his way to school, little boy walks up the gravel road ,dog entow, he bends down to wipe dust off his sneaks

The dog happy and frail, wagging his tail, runs out too close,

bus runs over the dog cracking his legs and his feet

Cold bitter winds of a snowy December, blast a blizzard as if where it hit was chosen

8 year old boy walks with his mama, so she could catch a ride to work,

He waits too long, and now his legs and feet are frozen

Tragedy strikes, a stolen soul, bold and cold like a thief in the night time

The dearly beloved rests in peace, while the travesty has left a mentally smashed family hammered in grief

He walks onto the top of the tallest building, too much to drink and can't think, like a lost cause and guilty

Helicopters hover over the building, he suddenly walks off, plummets down to a crowded street, a splattered grisly scene, now his end is filthy

Aggravated obliteration, reiteration of situations, sadistic amputation and decadent decapitation

M-16s, that chop as guillotines ,M-249s,Mach-11's, and Mossberg pumps, will make love to your frame as if it was the sweetest infatuation

A bad tooth in an infected gum, a crook in your neck, that can't be explained where it's from
Hot slug from a revolver, twists and turns through cartilage now it looks for an exit, when it never should have came out of the gun

Explicit lacerations with precision, with catastrophic conditions, and provisions made slim to none

a storm approaches, war encroaches again, you're warned to focus on movements and motion that's up close an intense

Car skids off an icy road, during a bad winter storm weather fog is dense

The passenger's seat belt protects him while the drivers ejected through the air like the sweet smell of the incense

For entertainment kids hopping around on an old mattress considered for garbage at the time

until one day, one of them has an idea of how to fly high, so he tries a backflip, in the air he went landing on his head severing his spine

giving love to someone, when you get no love back

, showing care with fear, knowing it could all blow up in your face like C4 before the attack

the longing of wanting someone special, the dreams and mental manifestations of making love taken to the next level

the waiting while incarcerated knowing you left a life out in the Free world.

From curiosity and concern, to the premonitions that burn.

The incarcerated thoughts that someone else could possibly be loving your girl

This is my visual perception of "PAIN"

Universal Reversal of Virtue"

Savage tactics
driving this country backwards
by cons, treaties and tea party theatrics

no real enemies,threat or actions
just genocidal homicide justified by governless horrific distractions
politicians political schemes now publicized by a random citizens
actions

P.O.T.U.S pissed off cuz his sneaky actions got snitched on

the masses theorize his affiliations to other worldly committees while
collecting commissions

2 Mannings played on a field throwing a football

but now known is the third one

dropping back he threw a long shot which reached the capitals head
murder 1
speaking of a murder done
Trayvon Martin
This is a race war,with a new Adolf starting
Nowadays I guess you can get killed for a hoody,skittles,and a juice
blue's clues who's who shoot young victim
who knew neighborhood shoots young men then
assailant unveiled jailed yells self-defense then

my mental is missing
kidnapped and defenseless

like a wild child running around no remedy
assassinations planned,plotted, and strategized
Evers,King,Kennedy

Viciously,for voicing opinionated opinions

delivering messages, at the discretion of those who was hired and
conspired to get rid of them

middle men, chosen for the dastardly deeds
hazardous disasterous antagonists fed lies to carry out the grisly scene
for unlimited green

this country has been a bully,full of perjury

and yet the ONLY place where murder is legally looked at as a service

only if you're in office,a blue collar politician,with a pension,and an
officially cleared purpose

I'm not a racist,but we all have been running a race

the race war is way more violent than Adolf
or more costlier than what Bernie Madoff

P.O.T.U.S and the government are puppets in this fascist controlled
NEW WORLD ORDER

where there's futuristic plans for mass hysteria herding us as cattle
for slaughter

young America walks around with eyes wide shut

symbolism not symbolic enough to simplistically stand up

make the perilous connection confessions not enough

in order for young America to foresee the pre-hysteria

before it's too late to navigate and deviate from these cannibals

yes animals but on 2 legs walking around no cage

just pretenders in suits and suspenders

sworn to carry out new agendas in this new age

deliverance from an unseen being is what we all await

the planet is severely damaged
thus sealing our fate

I fear for the tragedies of casualties and the assassinations maximized
in catastrophe

catastrophic numerical demise
will soon become rampant as a plague of locust clouding the sky

when the stars slowly descend and the sky opens up

the end of civilization will be evident

the prophecy will be fulfilled,a bright light in the sky will be seen by all near and far

a spectacle of perpetual conditions that will be amazing to all!!

"Deep Breath"

Stress is a test that's passed and failed

Many people never try to devise or prioritize their lives

In a manner where its simplified, so they won't prevail

Living in a world where problems and complications are all too common

To solve them is a resolve in which it takes time and may be even costly

An awesome division to add may multiply your life

So no one and nothing has to be subtracted while your evolving

Honestly life is just a chest game

I surmise in time

If the right moves are made, and your defense holds against the opposition

There will be nothing you can't accomplish

All it takes is faith and a vision...©

"The Real World ll"

Real eyes realize REAL lies!!!!

My country tis of thee

America is not a country

Its a business

Sweet land of liberty

In this land,this life,it costs to be free

Of thee I see

Cause I'm a witness to this

Genocidal fascist system
That we call a government

Well govern this,
where's all the money being spent
We don't own planes or sail no boats
But if we were Columbian
Bet we'd get escorted to the coast
To set up shop n sell coke

And why do anybody else get charges n prison sentences when caught
with what's suppose to be the worlds most dangerous drugs

when the govern less ,I mean government are the real drug dealers

only they wear suit n ties in front of the camera
but switch into the hoodies n tims later,they're the real thugs

When I think about what's going on in this business(country to some)

I'm terrified for my kids n for everyone else's kids,who have yet to see
the bigger picture
And have been stupified to be considered dumb

You know,Ima break it down to you

Ya see,the illuminations of the world illuminated for our boys n girls

are nothing more than a deception requested by those
Illuminated with hatred n hellbent on destruction n disruption

to any n everyone else,who are not in the celebrity n financially
blindfolded facade of a world I've stated

Bottom line,theyre concentrating on putting all of us in a camp,
where we don't sing songs,get along but rave and rant

we will then become nothing more than test subjects like rats in a cage

They figure, trap the body, n enslave the mind, to later on prep us to be mentally re- engraved

they've already started their diabolical plot

By attacking our children through music,fashion,fads,n any of the latest debatable plots

See I use to indulge in marijuana,but it just made me numb

But if ur dumbed down, when it comes down to your priorities n funds

then you've lost a war
That you never knew u were in,n your opponent,(the govern less) has already won!

And another thing,brothas need to stop showing their underclothes

 its not a fad,what's really goin on is,you've been had,

fooled into thinking its cool

just cause some young money rappers,or rappers with money thats young does it
its cool for me to follow

but the truth is its advertisement for some homosexuals to holla

Imagine if for every young brotha out there that wore their clothes that way, there was some gargantuan football player sized brutha that followed u everywhere,everyday

and no matter where you went, there was nothing u could do

and all your friends were going through the same thing too,

then what would u do,nonviolent to remedy the situation???

The right thing to do, would be to start dressing like you are a man n got some sense....

But who am I,I'm just a man who sees things differently from the rest of the world, n you should too!

These are real world warnings,so pay attention to the world around you!!!

America is not a country

Its a business n we r just the workers in the field all over again

Don't be dumbed down like fools n clowns

ain't no jokes being told, no reason to smile

If the truth is unbelievable, to those who hide

then why is it so easy to believe and be deceived by so many worldwide lies......©

"Blackout"

It's cold & dark, my cerebellum travels a million miles away mentally
surfing through brain waves, amidst the tides at Bay

Cemented inventions envisioned

Explicit in contradictions

Indicative to gun violence and school shootings through youthful
visions

Congratulations is in order for those that made it

From slums, hoods, and project buildings with or without a basement

Sharpened minds of the youth who's on the right side of worldly clarity

Leaders of a new age, construed and mentally infused with new ways
to remain in solidarity

For the rest of the youth to exert their energy

No more time to get paid motto, now it's build a business mentality

The fallacy of everyone is that were in the land of the free

Then why does everything costs, fresh water to drink or even the air that we breathe

Mask up to go into the world, these days seems like the new norm

Mask down, met with frowns no service to you in more than a few stores

This PLANdemic is nothing more than a damn gimmick

A systematic way to tighten a virtual noose around everyone's neck, a Klan mimic

The fate of the United Slaves Of America, is a grim one to never ignore

Some can't eat, can't sleep, some scream, "I can't breathe", r.i.p. to George Floyd

The years of oppression in transgression needs to stop

There must be a nation wide resistance in peaceful revision to be persistent in crime ridden spots

Police are paid, supposedly to protect and serve

Not to arrest in duress, and choke necks when stirred

Everyone in a law enforcement uniform needs monthly psych evaluations

So the Melanated number of murders can decline in maturation

Let's get back to basics, cause what were seeing is chaos in real time

Chaotic events, turned murder scenes to prints, becoming horrific movies right in front of our eyes

Who can speak for the ones we've lost

How do we connect with the families that's lost loved ones in thought

What's the number of tears we need to cry for the ones in power to get the point

We're sick and tired of it all we're being killed for no reason, and nothing seems to make a difference, to change any views to a point

Who then should we point the finger at, to give the blame to

The media, the politicians, the police, victims, the families, or is it more than these few

Someone recently told me, they were ready to have a baby in this day and age

They asked what I thought about it, I couldn't answer, my mind filled with rage, visualization of stages, profiling of races, competing in a race where last place is the start, part of your placement

With that being said, I just shook my head, and replied," to create a life is a gift, but to stay alive will be your greatest fight

The ending is near, the Apocalypse is the next bright light

Though this is the world we live in, feeling like an EMP has suddenly been destroyed and deployed as a cash cow

It's only a facade a macabre mirage, but the truth is scarier than fiction, for this is nothing more than a worldly "BLACKOUT"

CPSIA information can be obtained
at www.ICGtesting.com
Printed in the USA
BVHW031444030720
582914BV00001B/167